Bugs!

Shira Evans

NATIONAL
GEOGRAPHIC

Washington, D.C.

Vocabulary Tree

ANIMALS

BUGS

HOW BUGS LOOK

spots
stripes
short
wide
long
thin

WHAT BUGS HAVE

six legs
four wings
two antennae
sharp mouthparts

There are many kinds of bugs.
They live all around us.

Go outside and look.
Do you see any bugs?

Look closely at plants. You might see bugs on the leaves.

Some bugs have spots.

Other bugs have stripes.

Some bugs are short and wide.

Other bugs are long and thin.

All bugs have six legs.

abdomen

legs

Their bodies have three parts.

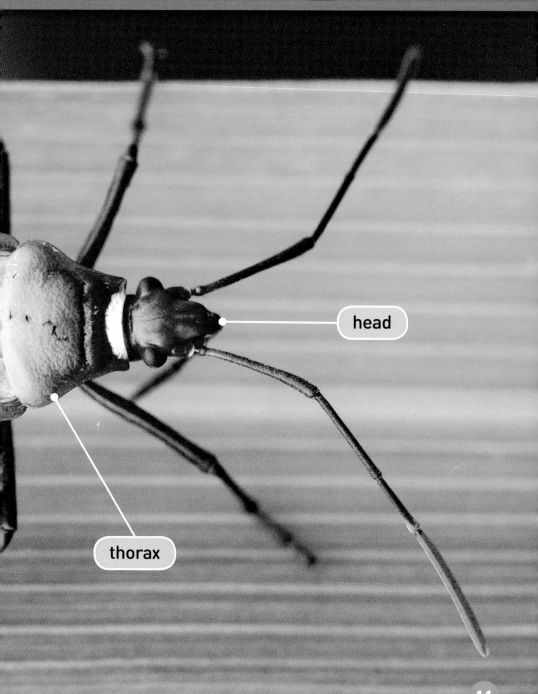

head

thorax

Bugs have two sets of wings.

wings

wings

They use their wings to fly.

Bugs have two long feelers, too.
Each feeler is called an antenna.

They tell the bug which way to go.

antennae

Bugs have sharp mouthparts.

mouthparts

They help the bug eat.

First the bug cuts into a plant.

Then the bug slurps up what's inside.

20

The spots can show that bugs are eating!

YOUR TURN!

Look at each bug.
Point to and say the name of
each body part you can see.

six legs   two antennae
four wings   sharp mouthparts

To Sam and Alex, whose love of the outdoors continues to inspire me. —S.E.

NOTE FROM THE AUTHOR:
All bugs are insects, but not all insects are bugs. The word "bug" refers to one order of insects called Hemiptera. These are known as true bugs. True bugs have sucking mouthparts and two sets of wings (one a hard shell and one soft for flying). Like all insects, they have six legs and three body parts.

The bugs pictured in this book include:
- Bee assassin bug
- Lantern bug
- Shield bug
- Italian striped bug
- Blue stink bug
- Capsid bug
- Red cotton stainer bug
- Large brown cicada
- Leaf-footed bug
- Dock bug
- Hibiscus harlequin bug
- Thread-legged bug

The publisher gratefully acknowledges the expert content review of this book by Dr. William O. Lamp, University of Maryland, Department of Entomology, and the expert literacy review of this book by Kimberly Gillow, principal, Milan Area Schools, Michigan.

Designed by Sanjida Rashid

Photo Credits
Cover, Ingo Arndt/Minden Pictures; 1, Chaikom/Shutterstock; 2-3, Anake Seenadee/Shutterstock; 4-5, real444/Getty Images; 6, Mitsuhiko Imamori/Minden Pictures; 7, InsectWorld/Shutterstock; 8, Ruzy Hartini/Shutterstock; 9, Cisca Castelijns/NiS/Minden Pictures; 10-11, yod67/Getty Images; 12, Mitsuhiko Imamori/Minden Pictures; 13, Satoshi Kuribayashi/Minden Pictures; 14-15, Ingo Arndt/Minden Pictures; 16-17, PBWPIX/Alamy Stock Photo; 18-19, Radu Bercan/Shutterstock; 20, CarloneGiovanni/Getty Images; 21, AlasdairJames/Getty Images; 22, Sam Fraser-Smith; 23 (UP), KozyrevAnton/Getty Images; 23 (LO), bluehand/Shutterstock; 24, Narupon Nimpaiboon/Shutterstock

Library of Congress Cataloging-in-Publication Data

Names: Evans, Shira, author. | National Geographic Society (U.S.)
Title: Bugs / by Shira Evans.
Description: Washington, DC : National Geographic Kids, [2018] | Series: National geographic readers | Audience: Ages 2-5. | Audience: Preschool excluding K.
Identifiers: LCCN 2017050046 (print) | LCCN 2017058647 (ebook) | ISBN 9781426330322 (ebook) | ISBN 9781426330339 (ebook + audio) | ISBN 9781426330308 (pbk.) | ISBN 9781426330315 (hardcover)
Subjects: LCSH: Hemiptera--Juvenile literature. | Insects--Juvenile literature.
Classification: LCC QL521 (ebook) | LCC QL521 .E93 2018 (print) | DDC595.7/52--dc23
LC record available at https://lccn.loc.gov/2017050046

National Geographic supports K–12 educators with ELA Common Core Resources. Visit natgeoed.org/commoncore for more information.

Printed in the United States of America
18/WOR/1